11|3|14

The Age of Dinosaurs

Meet Plateosaurus

Written by Henley Miller

Illustrations by Leonello Calvetti and Luca Massini

 Cavendish
Square

New York

Published in 2015 by Cavendish Square Publishing, LLC
243 5th Avenue, Suite 136, New York, NY 10016

Website: cavendishsq.com

This publication represents the opinions and views of the author based on his or her personal experience, knowledge, and research. The information in this book serves as a general guide only. The author and publisher have used their best efforts in preparing this book and disclaim liability rising directly or indirectly from the use and application of this book.

CPSIA Compliance Information: Batch #WS14CSQ

All websites were available and accurate when this book was sent to press.

Library of Congress Cataloging-in-Publication Data

Miller, Henley, author.
Meet Plateosaurus / Henley Miller.
pages cm. — (The age of dinosaurs)
Includes bibliographical references and index.
ISBN 978-1-62712-797-4 (hardcover) ISBN 978-1-62712-798-1 (paperback) ISBN 978-1-62712-799-8 (ebook)
1. Plateosaurus—Juvenile literature. I. Title.

QE862.S3M55 2015
567.913—dc23

2014001527

Editorial Director: Dean Miller
Copy Editor: Cynthia Roby
Art Director: Jeffrey Talbot
Designer: Douglas Brooks
Photo Researcher: J8 Media
Production Manager: Jennifer Ryder-Talbot
Production Editor: David McNamara
Illustrations by Leonello Calvetti and Luca Massini

The photographs in this book are used by permission and through the courtesy of:
gkuna/iStock/Thinkstock, 8; peter zelei/E+/Getty Images, 8; © ZUMA Press, Inc./Alamy, 20;
FunkMonk/File:Plateosaurus MSF23.jpg/Wikimedia Commons, 21;
Ghedoghedo/File:Plateosaurus engelharti.jpg/Wikimedia Commons, 21.

Printed in the United States of America

CONTENTS

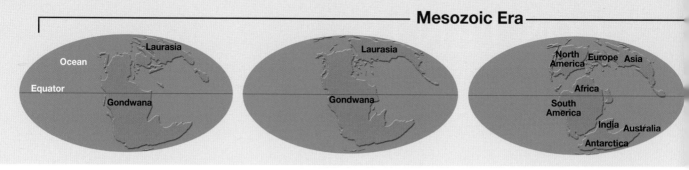

Late Triassic
206 – 227 million years ago.

Early Jurassic
206 –176 million years ago.

Middle Jurassic
176 – 159 million years ago.

A CHANGING WORLD

Earth's long history began 4.6 billion years ago. Dinosaurs were among the most fascinating life forms from Earth's long past.

The word "dinosaur" originates from the Greek words *deinos* and *sauros*, which together mean "fearfully great lizards."

To understand dinosaurs we need to understand geological time, the lifetime of our planet. Earth's history is divided into eras, periods, epochs, and ages. The dinosaur era, called the Mesozoic era,

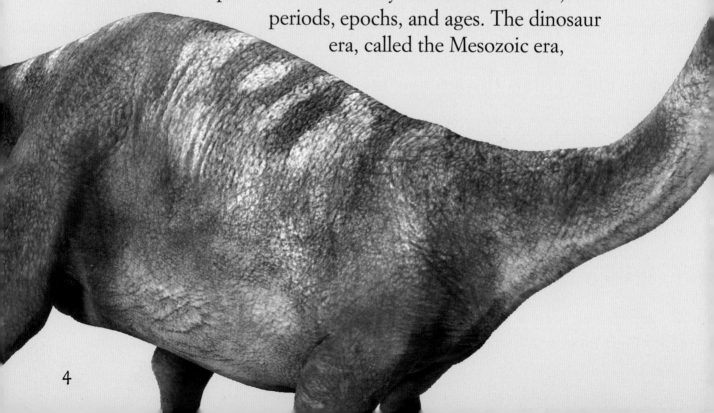

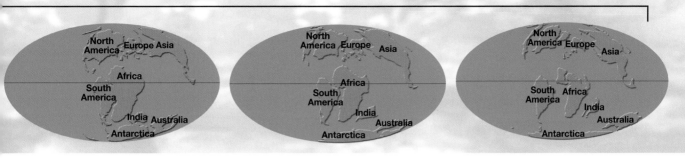

Late Jurassic	Early Cretaceous	Late Cretaceous
159 – 144 million years ago.	144 – 99 million years ago.	99 – 65 million years ago.

is divided in three periods: Triassic, which lasted 42 million years; Jurassic, 61 million years; and Cretaceous, 79 million years. Dinosaurs ruled the world for 160 million years.

Man and dinosaurs never met. This is because dinosaurs had become extinct nearly 65 million years before man's appearance on Earth.

The dinosaur world differed from our world. The climate was warmer, the continents were different, and grass did not even exist!

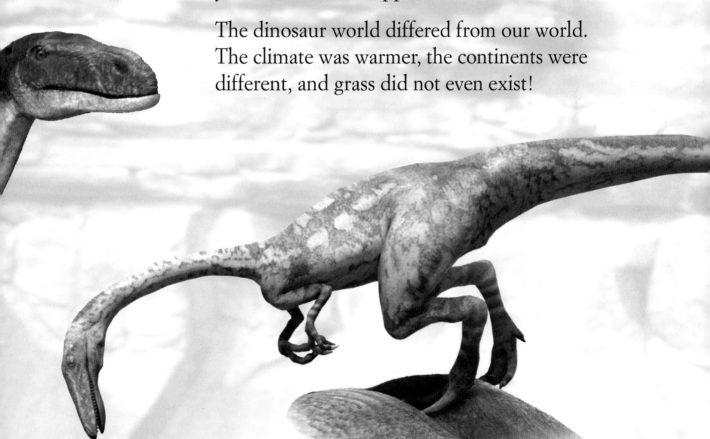

A LONG, FLAT DINOSAUR

Plateosaurus (pronounced PLAY-tee-uh-SAWR-us) was a Saurischian dinosaur belonging to the order *Saurischia*, meaning "lizard-hipped," and the infra-order *Prosauropoda*, meaning "before the lizard-footed." These orders roamed Earth in herds during the Late Triassic and Early Jurassic periods between 180 and 225 million years ago. Plateosaurus lived on the continent known today as Europe.

The name Plateosaurus comes from the Greek word meaning "flat lizard." This is likely because some parts of its skeleton appear flat. German paleontologist Herbert von Meyer, who gave the dinosaur its name, never explained why he chose it.

A large-bellied dinosaur, Plateosaurus had a long tail; long hind limbs, or back legs; and short forelegs, or front legs. Its head was small with a beak-shaped jaw structure. Its rough-edged teeth were shaped like diamonds. The male Plateosaurus could measure up to 29 feet (9 meters) long, 10–13 feet (3–4 m) high, and weigh as much as 8,000 pounds (3,629 kilograms). Although the females may have been a little smaller, the Plateosaurus remains among the largest terrestrial animals in the Triassic period.

FINDING PLATEOSAURUS

Plateosaurus roamed about the countries of Germany, Switzerland, and France. The dinosaur preferred the dry, almost desert-like environment of Europe. During the Late Triassic period, 203–205 million years ago, Plateosaurus lived in Greenland.

Plateosaurus was the largest and most common dinosaur of its time. It was more massive than earlier dinosaurs and had bones that were stocky and thick. Only two species of this dinosaur are known: *Plateosaurus longiceps*, the most common, and *Plateosaurus engelhardti*.

Germany

France

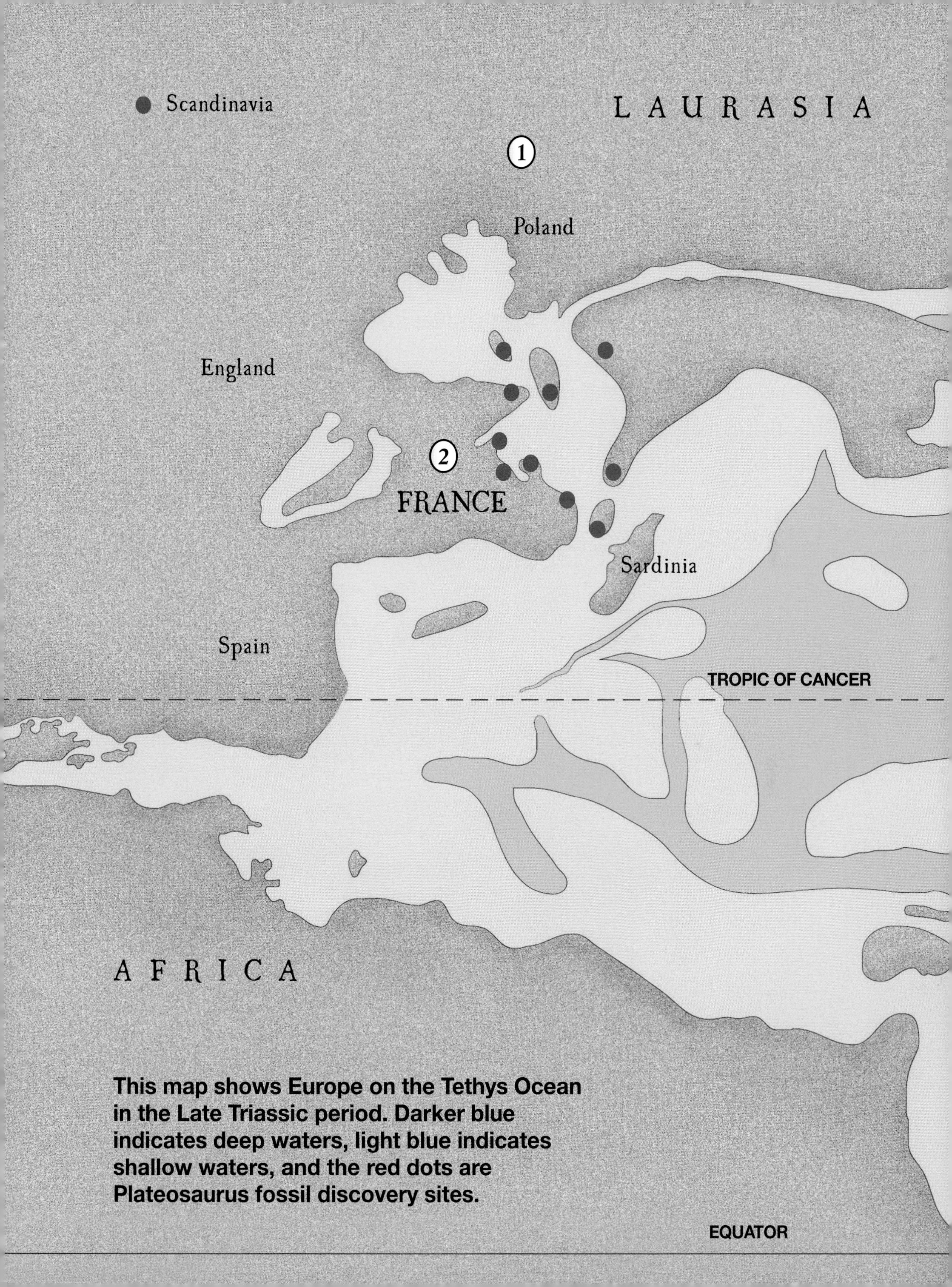

Scandinavia

L A U R A S I A

①

Poland

England

②

FRANCE

Sardinia

Spain

TROPIC OF CANCER

A F R I C A

This map shows Europe on the Tethys Ocean in the Late Triassic period. Darker blue indicates deep waters, light blue indicates shallow waters, and the red dots are Plateosaurus fossil discovery sites.

EQUATOR

YOUNG PLATEOSAURUS

No Plateosaurus eggs or nests have been unearthed during fossil excavations, so little is known about baby Plateosaurs. What paleontologists do know is that the greatest dangers baby Plateosaurus faced were the small carnivorous, or meat-eating, dinosaurs that roamed the area on the lookout for an easy dinner. Plateosaurus parents were protective of their young. When the dinosaurs traveled or rested, young Plateosaurus always remained on the inside, encircled by members of the herd.

STOMACH OF STONE

Because of Plateosaurus' massive-sized body, it certainly had to consume large amounts of food to be satisfied. Yet the dinosaur had one problem: the jagged edges of its teeth. Although perfect for tearing at the plants and leaves it loved to eat, the dinosaur's teeth were not suited to grind food for digestion. It swallowed small rocks to help the process. These rocks, called "stomach stones," moved around inside Plateosaurus' stomach, smashing the large chunks of swallowed food into pulp.

MEALTIME

Plateosaurs were the first-known large herbivores among the dinosaurs. Their diet was mainly tender plants such as leaves, fruits, and buds. The dinosaurs used their powerful, clawed hands to pull down, and feed on, heavy leaves or stems that stored water. If given the opportunity, Plateosaurs may have captured a small animal or predator near their herd. Paleontologists feel that, in a sense, the plateosaurs were also omnivorous, or eager to eat both plants and animals.

TREACHEROUS WATERS

Low and muddy lakes were scattered throughout the Triassic flood plains where herds of plateosaurs roamed. During the Triassic period, these lakes acted as wet, spongy earth. Paleontologists believe that plateosaurs came to these areas to feed on the plants. While searching for food, some of the larger plateosaurs became stuck in the mud. The dinosaurs tried to free themselves but could not. The more they struggled, the deeper they sank. Tired, they eventually collapsed. Some starved to death. Several plateosaurs over the years became stuck in the same areas. This is why paleontologists were able to unearth a great number of the dinosaurs' complete skeletons.

INSIDE PLATEOSAURUS

Plateosaurus' long forelimbs suggest that it walked on four legs, but on occasion raised itself up to run on its hind limbs alone. Its forefoot had five digits, or fingers. Its hind limbs had four clawed toes with a fifth toe that was nothing more than a stub. The skull was small. The lower and upper jawbones held from twenty-seven to thirty-five small diamond-shaped teeth. A long neck permitted Plateosaurus to graze high up in the trees.

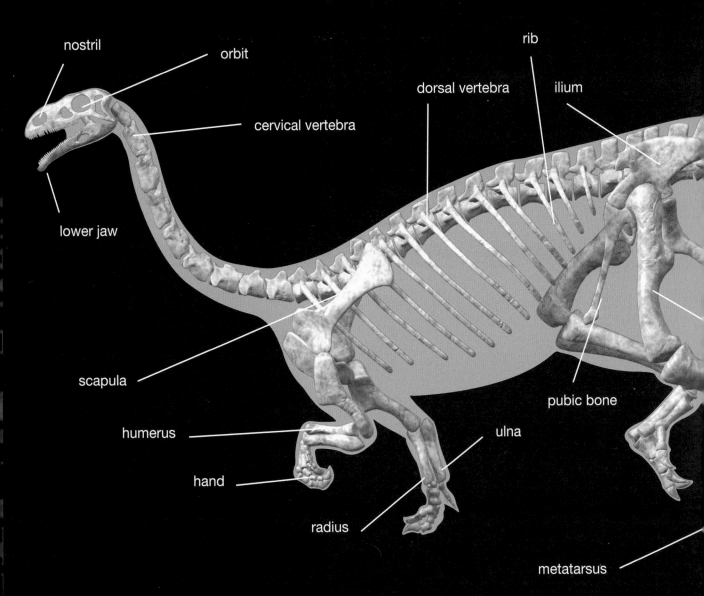

nostril

orbit

rib

dorsal vertebra

ilium

cervical vertebra

lower jaw

scapula

pubic bone

humerus

ulna

hand

radius

metatarsus

Side view of the skull

Dorsal view of the skull

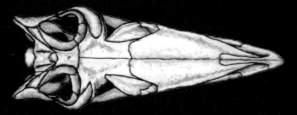

View of the lower jaw

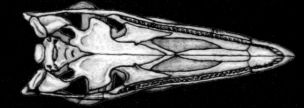

caudal vertebra

chevron

ischium

femur

tibia

thumb

foot

bones and claws of the foot

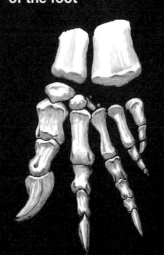

bones and claws of the hand

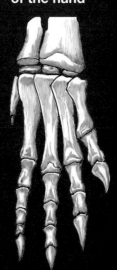

UNEARTHING PLATEOSAURUS

Many complete Plateosaurus skeletons have been unearthed from more than fifty different sites throughout Europe and Greenland. In 1906, a large deposit of Plateosaurus bones near Trossingen, Germany, was discovered. From 1911 to 1912, paleontologists from the Museum of Natural History of Stuttgart carried out the excavations.

From 1921–1923, and then in 1932, other paleontologists from the University of Tübingen took part in the excavations, and more than fifty complete skeletons were unearthed in areas where Plateosaurs had been trapped in the mud.

A complete skeleton of an adult Plateosaurus.

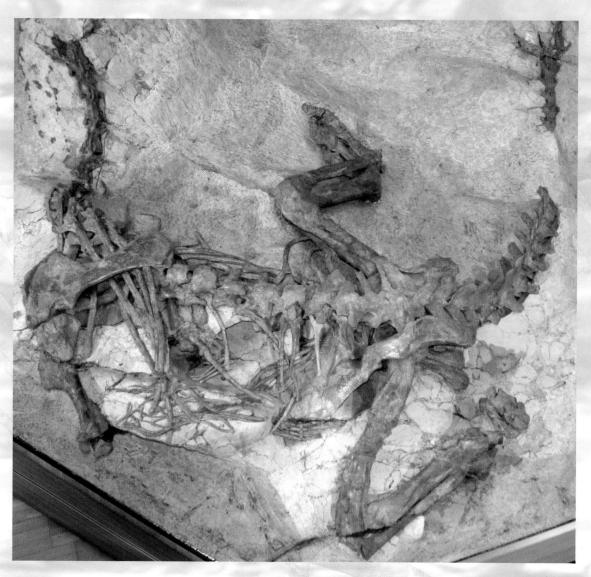

Plateosaurus engelhardti displayed at the Sauriermuseum Frick in Switzerland.

A close-up of a Plateosaurus skull.

THE PROSAUROPODS

The discovery sites of the prosauropods are depicted here.

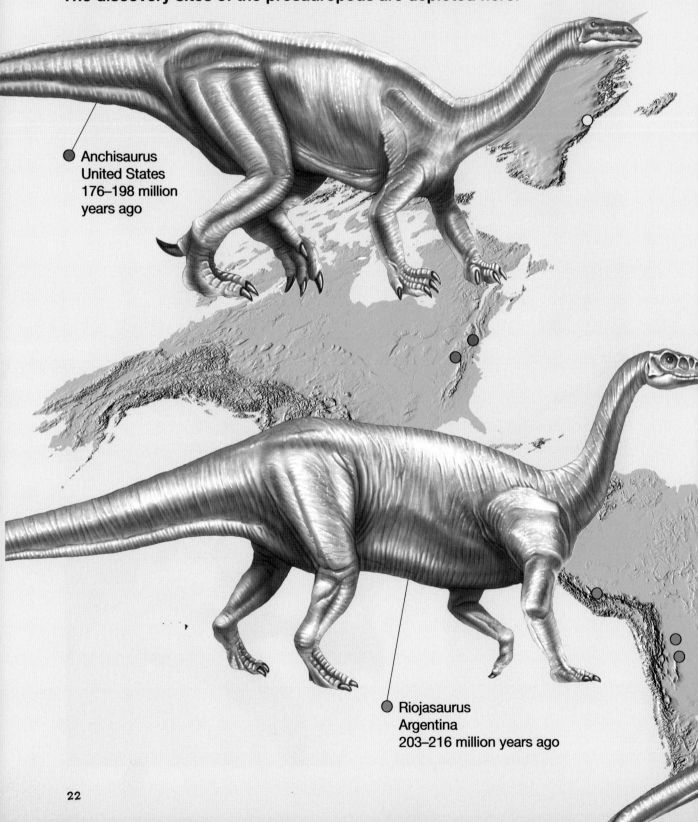

Anchisaurus
United States
176–198 million
years ago

Riojasaurus
Argentina
203–216 million years ago

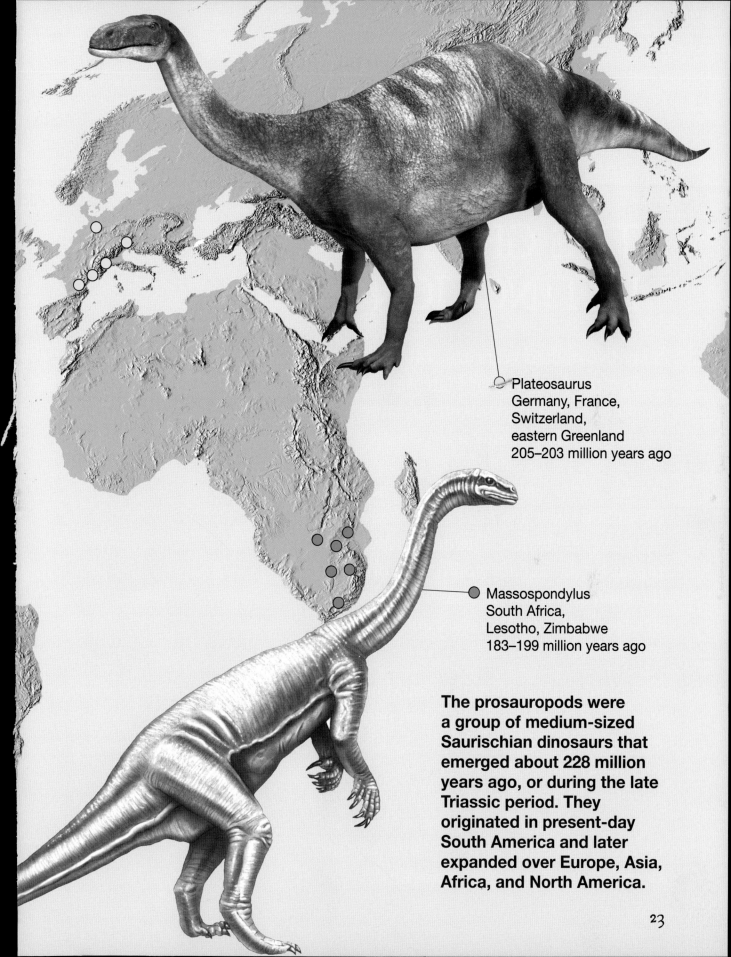

Plateosaurus
Germany, France,
Switzerland,
eastern Greenland
205–203 million years ago

Massospondylus
South Africa,
Lesotho, Zimbabwe
183–199 million years ago

The prosauropods were
a group of medium-sized
Saurischian dinosaurs that
emerged about 228 million
years ago, or during the late
Triassic period. They
originated in present-day
South America and later
expanded over Europe, Asia,
Africa, and North America.

THE GREAT EXTINCTION

Sixty-five million years ago, 140 million years after the time that Plateosaurus roamed the Earth, dinosaurs became extinct. Scientists think a large meteorite hitting the Earth caused this extinction. A wide crater caused by a meteorite exactly 65 million years ago has been located along the coast of Mexico. The dust suspended in the air by the impact would have obscured the sunlight for a long time, causing a drastic drop in temperature and killing many plants.

The plant-eating dinosaurs would have starved or frozen to death. Meat-eating dinosaurs would have also died without their food supply. However, some scientists believe dinosaurs did not die out completely and that present-day chickens and other birds are, in a way, the descendants of the large dinosaurs.

A DINOSAUR'S FAMILY TREE

The oldest dinosaur fossils are 220–225 million years old and have been found all over the world.

Dinosaurs are divided into two groups. Saurischians are similar to reptiles, with the pubic bone directed forward, while the Ornithischians are like birds, with the pubic bone directed backward.

Saurischians are subdivided in two main groups: Sauropodomorphs, to which quadrupeds and vegetarians belong; and Theropods, which include bipeds and predators.

Ornithischians are subdivided into three large groups: Thyreophorans, which include the quadrupeds Stegosaurians and Ankylosaurians; Ornithopods; and Marginocephalians, which are subdivided into the bipedal Pachycephalosaurians and the mainly quadrupedal Ceratopsians.

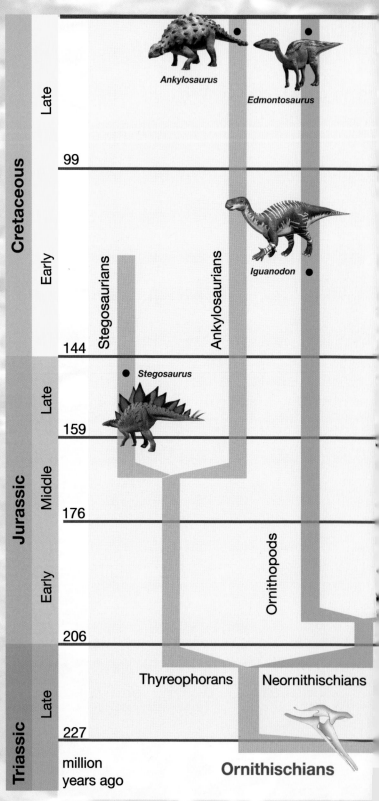

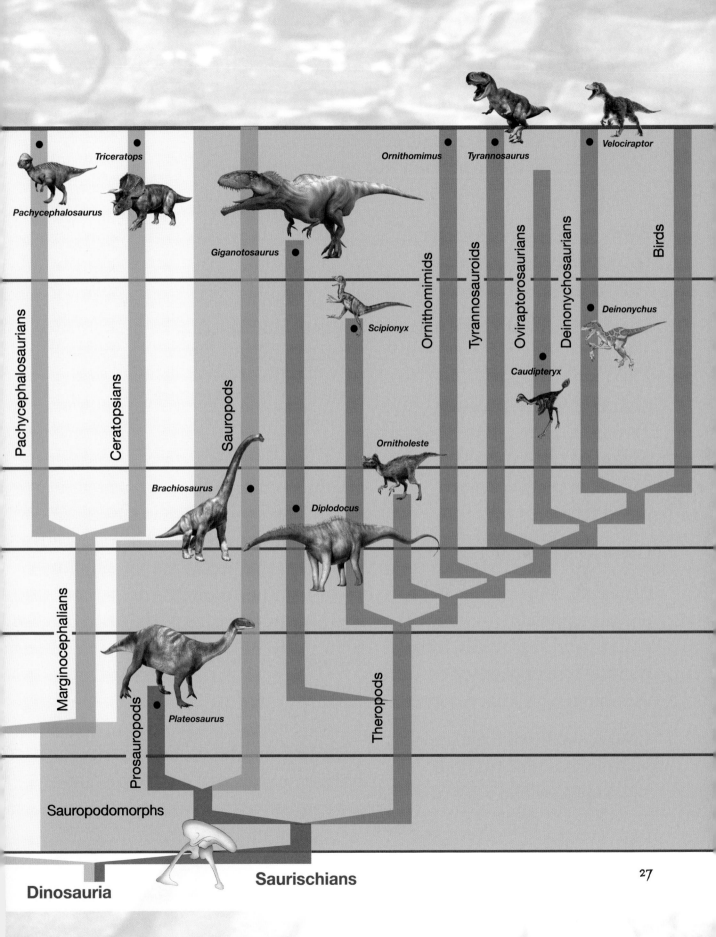

Pachycephalosaurians

Ceratopsians

Marginocephalians

Prosauropods

Sauropodomorphs

Dinosauria

Pachycephalosaurus

Triceratops

Giganotosaurus

Sauropods

Brachiosaurus

Diplodocus

Plateosaurus

Scipionyx

Ornitholeste

Theropods

Ornithomimids

Ornithomimus

Tyrannosauroids

Tyrannosaurus

Oviraptorosaurians

Caudipteryx

Deinonychosaurians

Velociraptor

Deinonychus

Birds

Saurischians

A SHORT VOCABULARY OF DINOSAURS

Bipedal: pertaining to an animal moving on two feet alone, almost always those of the hind legs.

Bone: hard tissue made mainly of calcium phosphate; single element of the skeleton.

Carnivore: a meat-eating animal.

Caudal: pertaining to the tail.

Cenozoic Era (Caenozoic, Tertiary Era): the interval of geological time between 65 million years ago and present day.

Cervical: pertaining to the neck.

Claws: the fingers and toes of predator animals end with pointed and sharp nails, called claws. Those of plant-eaters end with blunt nails, called hooves.

Cretaceous Period: the interval of geological time between 144 and 65 million years ago.

Egg: a large cell enclosed in a porous shell produced by reptiles and birds to reproduce themselves.

Epoch: a memorable date or event.

Evolution: changes in the character states of organisms, species, and higher ranks through time.

Extinct: when something, such as a species of animal, is no longer existing.

Feathers: outgrowth of the skin of birds and some dinosaurs, used in flight and in providing insulation and protection for the body. They evolved from reptilian scales.

Forage: to wander in search of food.

Fossil: evidence of life in the past. Not only bones, but footprints and trails made by animals, as well as dung, eggs or plant resin, when fossilized, are fossils.

Herbivore: a plant-eating animal.

Jurassic Period: the interval of geological time between 206 and 144 million years ago.

Mesozoic Era (**Mesozoic, Secondary Era**): the interval of geological time between 248 and 65 million years ago.

Pack: a group of predator animals acting together to capture their prey.

Paleontologist: a scientist who studies and reconstructs the prehistoric life.

Paleozoic Era (**Paleozoic, Primary Era**): the interval of geological time between 570 and 248 million years ago.

Predator: an animal that preys on other animals for food.

Raptor (**raptorial**): a bird of prey, such as an eagle, hawk, falcon, or owl.

Rectrix (**plural rectrices**): any of the larger feathers in a bird's tail that are important in helping its flight direction.

Scavenger: an animal that eats dead animals.

Skeleton: a structure of an animal's body made of several different bones. One primary function is to protect delicate organs such as the brain, lungs, and heart.

Skin: the external, thin layer of the animal body. Skin cannot fossilize, unless it is covered by scales, feathers, or fur.

Skull: bones that protect the brain and the face.

Teeth: tough structures in the jaws used to hold, cut, and sometimes process food.

Terrestrial: living on land.

Triassic Period: the interval of geological time between 248 and 206 million years ago.

Unearth: to find something that was buried beneath the earth.

Vertebrae: the single bones of the backbone; they protect the spinal cord.

DINOSAUR WEBSITES

Dino Database
www.dinodatabase.com
Get the latest news on dinosaur research and discoveries.
This site is pretty advanced, so you may need help from a teacher
or parent to find what you're looking for.

Dinosaurs for Kids
www.kidsdinos.com
There's basic information about most dinosaur types, and you can
play dinosaur games, vote for your favorite dinosaur, and learn
about the study of dinosaurs, paleontology.

Dinosaur Train
pbskids.org/dinosaurtrain
From the PBS show *Dinosaur Train*, you can watch videos,
print out pages to color, play games, and learn lots of facts about
so many dinosaurs!

Discovery Channel Dinosaur Videos
discovery.com/video-topics/other/other-topics-dinosaur-videos.htm
Watch almost 100 videos about the life of dinosaurs!

The Natural History Museum
www.nhm.ac.uk/kids-only/dinosaurs
Take a quiz to see how much you know about dinosaurs—or a quiz
to tell you what type of dinosaur you'd be! There's also
a fun directory of dinosaurs, including some cool 3-D views of
your favorites.

MUSEUMS

American Museum of Natural History, New York, NY
www.amnh.org

Carnegie Museum of Natural History, Pittsburgh, PA
www.carnegiemnh.org

Denver Museum of Nature and Science, Denver, CO
www.dmns.org

Dinosaur National Monument, Dinosaur, CO
www.nps.gov/dino

The Field Museum, Chicago, IL
fieldmuseum.org

University of California Museum of Paleontology, Berkeley, CA
www.ucmp.berkeley.edu

Museum of the Rockies, Bozeman, MT
www.museumoftherockies.org

National Museum of Natural History, Smithsonian Institution,
Washington, DC
www.mnh.si.edu

Royal Tyrrell Museum of Palaeontology, Drumheller, Canada
www.tyrrellmuseum.com

Sam Noble Museum of Natural History, Norman, OK
www.snomnh.ou.edu

Yale Peabody Museum of Natural History, New Haven, CT
peabody.yale.edu

INDEX

Page numbers in **boldface** are illustrations.